WELCOME TO MY COUNTRY

Welcome to
BANGLADESH

FRANKLIN WATTS
LONDON·SYDNEY

This edition first published in 2006 by
Franklin Watts
338 Euston Road
London NW1 3BH

This edition is published for sale only in the United Kingdom and Eire.

© Marshall Cavendish International (Asia) Pte Ltd 2006
Originated and designed by Times Editions–Marshall Cavendish
An imprint of Marshall Cavendish International (Asia) Pte Ltd
1 New Industrial Road, Singapore 536196

Written by: Eileen Khoo
Designer: Cynthia Ng
Picture researchers: Thomas Khoo & Joshua Ang

A CIP catalogue record for this book
is available from the British Library.

ISBN-10: 0 7496 7015 0
ISBN-13: 978 0 7496 7015 3

Printed in Malaysia

Franklin Watts is a division of Hachette Children's Books.

Acknowledgements: The publishers would
like to thank Mohammad Shams-Ul Islam,
CEO/Director of Agrani Exchange House
Private Limited (An Exchange House owned
by AGRANI BANK, Bangladesh), for the
loan and use of his samples of Bangladeshi
currency in this book.

PICTURE CREDITS
Agence France Presse: 14, 15, 17, 27 (top),
    36, 37, 38, 39
alt.TYPE/Reuters: 19, 26, 27 (both)
Bes Stock: 9, 21. 43
The Bridgeman Art Library: 11
Eye Ubiquitous/Hutchinson: 30
Haga Library, Japan: 3 (top), 31
The Hutchison Picture Library: 1, 4, 6, 7,
    24, 32, 45
Jason Laure: cover, 20
Ellen London: 28, 33, 35
Lonely Planet Images: 3 (bottom), 18
North Wind Picture Archives: 12
Photolibrary.com: 3 (centre), 8
David Simson: 2, 22, 40, 41
Liba Taylor: 5, 23, 25, 34
Topham Picturepoint: 13, 16, 29

Digital Scanning by Superskill Graphics Pte Ltd

Contents

Words that appear in the glossary are printed in **bold** the first time they occur in the text.

Welcome to Bangladesh!

Bangladesh is located in South Asia. It is home to the Royal Bengal tiger and to the Sundarbans, the world's longest belt of mangrove trees. Bangladesh is one of the most crowded and poorest countries in the world. Let's explore Bangladesh and learn about its people!

Opposite: The roads near Dhaka's wharf are always bustling with pedestrians, trishaws and ferries.

Below: These people in northern Bangladesh travel in a large boat to get from one side of a river to the other.

The Flag of Bangladesh

On Bangladesh's flag, the red circle stands for the people who died during Bangladesh's fight for freedom. It is also for the "rising sun of a new country". The green is for the country's official religion, Islam, and for rich plant life.

The Land

Bangladesh is bordered by India to the west, north and east. Myanmar is to the southeast. The Bay of Bengal is to the south. Plains cover most of the nation. The rest of the country is covered in lakes, swamps, marshes and two hilly areas, the Sylhet Hills and the Chittagong Hill Tracts. Keokradong, in the Chittagong Hill Tracts, is the nation's highest peak. It stands 1,230 metres high.

Below: More and more people are coming to live in the city of Dhaka. It is becoming overcrowded.

Rivers, Plains and Deltas

The Ganges, the Brahmaputra and the Meghna are Bangladesh's three main rivers. They divide the nation into many plains and **deltas**. The Barind Tract is in the far northwest. The Jamuna Flood Plains, the Bhar **Basin**, the Madhupur Tract and the Northeastern Lowland are in the north. The Meghna Flood Basin is in central Bangladesh. In the southeast are the Central Delta Basins. Bangladesh has more than 8,045 kilometres of waterways. Many Bangladeshis travel by boat.

Above:
The beach near the town of Cox's Bazar has become popular with tourists. It is about 120 kilometres long.

Climate

Bangladesh has a **subtropical** climate. It has three main seasons. The winter season is mild and damp and lasts from October to March. Summer is hot and damp and lasts from March to June. The **monsoon** season is from June to October. In early summer and late in the monsoon season, the country has heavy thunderstorms and high winds, which can blow at more than 160 kilometres per hour. The storms and winds often cause tidal waves as high as 6 metres. The waves crash into the southern coast and islands offshore.

Left: The shapla (SHAH-PLAH), or water lily, is the national flower of Bangladesh. It blooms during the warm months of the year.

Plants and Animals

Bangladesh is home to subtropical and tropical plants, including fruit trees such as mango, betel nut and coconut trees. The large mangrove forests of the Sundarbans grow in the south. Flowers, such as marigolds, flame-of-the-forest and lotus jasmine, grow in Bangladesh.

Many kinds of animals live in the country, including Royal Bengal tigers, elephants, water buffalo and Malayan sun bears. Birds in the country include cuckoos, parakeets and woodpeckers.

History

As early as 1000 BCE, the Bang people lived in what is now Bangladesh. From 320 to 180 BCE, the Mauryan **Empire** ruled all of what is now India, Pakistan and Bangladesh. Later, eastern Bengal, which is now Bangladesh, became the separate kingdom of Samatata. It was ruled by the Gupta Empire of India. In 606 CE, the Harsha Empire took over. Under their rule, eastern Bengal was mostly ignored and uncared for.

The Palas to the Delhi Sultanate

From 750 to 1150, the region was ruled by the Pala **Dynasty**. Under the Palas, the Buddhist religion spread, and the region was peaceful. In 1150, the Senas took control. Under their harsh rule, a **caste** system was put in place. In the late 1100s, Turkish warriors took over. Under their rule, most people became followers of the Islamic religion. The Delhi Sultanate ruled most of Bengal and regions around it until the 1500s.

Opposite: In 1576, Akbar the Great *(top row, centre)*, ruler of the Mughal Empire, took over much of Bengal. Generals were sent to Bengal to take control and serve as governors. By the 1700s, the governors of Bengal had begun to take more and more control away from the Mughal rulers.

Left: This illustration shows fighting between Indian soldiers and British troops during the Great Mutiny of 1857. The Mutiny was caused by the people's unhappiness with the East India Company. After the Mutiny, India was ruled directly by Britain.

British Rule

Many Europeans, mostly from Britain, began to settle in South Asia in the late 1400s. In 1600, the East India Company was formed with the support of Britain. The East India Company worked to get Mughal governors to sign special trade agreements. By the 1850s, the company controlled most of what is now India, Pakistan and Bangladesh.

In 1858, the Mughal governors were officially taken out of power. Britain then took over the lands that were once controlled by the East India Company. They named the region "British India".

Two Pakistans

In 1947, British India was divided into India and Pakistan. Pakistan had two parts. East Pakistan (now Bangladesh) was separated from West Pakistan (now Pakistan) by India. The two Pakistans had different cultures and languages. Fighting broke out after West Pakistan tried to make its language, Urdu, the language of both parts of Pakistan.

Left: A British man oversees a group of Bengal people making tea boxes. At first, the British controlled Bengal's economy. After the land was divided, West Pakistan took over the region's economy, military and government. The unfair division made people in East Pakistan angry.

Left: In April 2003, Sri Lankan president Chandrika Kumaratunga *(centre)* visited Dhaka for two days. She met with Bangladeshi president Iajuddin Ahmed *(left)* and Bangladeshi prime minister Begum Khaleda Zia *(right)* during her visit.

The Liberation War and After

In 1971, after 20 years of fighting between East and West Pakistan, the Pakistan Army entered East Pakistan. They killed more than 100,000 people. India joined the **Liberation** War to stop the killing, and West Pakistan gave up.

In 1971, while a prisoner in Pakistan, Sheikh Mujib was named Bangladesh's first president. He was killed in 1975. In 1976, Major Ziaur Rahman, known as Zia, took over. In 1981, he was killed as well. In 1982, Lieutenant General Hussain Muhammad Ershad used force to take control. In 1990, many people argued against him, so he left office.

Asoka (273–232 BCE)

Asoka was a famous Mauryan ruler. His rule was harsh at first. He became a follower of Buddhism, which teaches kindness. After that, he did good deeds, such as building hospitals for animals.

Akbar the Great (1556–1605)

Akbar the Great was the most respected ruler of the Mughal Empire. He became emperor when he was just 13 years old. Akbar believed in equal rights for all men. He was able to unite groups of people in his empire who had fought for a long time. He helped the Mughal Empire grow strong and wealthy.

Sheikh Hasina Wajed (1947–)

Sheikh Hasina Wajed

The daughter of President Mujib, Sheikh Hasina Wajed was forced to flee the country after her father and family were killed. In 1981, she came back. She later served two terms in parliament. She became Bangladesh's second female prime minister in 1996.

Government and the Economy

Bangladesh's government has three branches. The executive branch makes rules for the government and also runs it. It is led by the president, the prime minister and a cabinet, or group of advisers. The prime minister, not the president, runs most of the government.

Below: Men walk past Bangladesh's parliament building. It was designed by American architect Louis Isadore Khan (1901–1974).

Left: President Iajuddin Ahmed *(left, front)* stands at attention at a ceremony on Independence Day 2003. Standing with him are then Army Chief Lieutenant General Hasa Mashhud Chowdhury *(left, back)*, then Navy Chief Admiral Shah Iqbal Muztaba *(centre)*, and Air Force Chief Vice Marshal Fakhru Azam *(right)*.

The **legislative** branch in Bangladesh is a one-house parliament called the Jatiya Sangsad, or National Parliament. It has 300 elected members.

The judiciary branch is headed by the Supreme Court. It oversees a system of lower courts, including the High Court Division and **Appellate** Division.

Bangladesh's land is divided into six regions: Chittagong, Barisal, Rajshahi, Khulna, Dhaka and Sylhet. Each region is divided into *zilla* (JEH-lah), which are districts. The zilla are then divided into groups of villages, which are called *thana* (THAH-nah).

The Economy

Many people in Bangladesh cannot find jobs. Often, they go to countries such as Saudi Arabia, Singapore, Kuwait and Malaysia to work. Service industries in Bangladesh produce half of all earnings each year. Bangladesh's most important natural resources are good soil, natural gas and oil. India and other countries have tried to get Bangladesh to **export** natural gas. Government officials have refused. They want the energy needs of Bangladeshis to be met first.

Left: This man is harvesting jute. Bangladesh is one of the largest producers of jute in the world. Today, the demand for jute is low. Many of the items that used to be made of jute, such as bags, are now made from plastic.

Left: Two women dry fish in the district of Cox's Bazar. Many kinds of fish and other seafood are caught in the waters near Cox's Bazar and are then frozen for export.

Farming and Other Industries

Many Bangladeshis work in farming. They mainly grow rice, sugarcane, tea, wheat, potatoes, spices, pulses and fruits. Most of the crops grown are used to feed Bangladeshis, not for export.

Many industries in Bangladesh are related to farming, including processing crops such as jute, sugarcane and tea. The country's most important industry, however, is making clothes for export. Industries in Bangladesh also produce paper, cement and fertilisers.

People and Lifestyle

Almost all Bangladeshis are **ethnic** Bengalis. A few people are from other ethnic groups. Bangladeshis who follow the Hindu religion are divided into social classes called castes. The laws of the caste determine a person's rights, who his or her friends can be and also whom he or she can marry. Muslims, or followers of Islam, have social classes, too. Today, social class is based more on a person's job, how much land he or she owns and his or her education.

Left: A Muslim girl *(second from right)* poses with her three Hindu friends. Both Muslims and Hindus have social classes.

Families

In Bangladesh, the **traditional** family unit is called a *poribar* (POH-ree-bar). A poribar includes parents, unmarried children and married sons and their families. The oldest man is head of the poribar. The oldest woman is respected as well. A poribar may live in the same house or in a group of houses. Some unmarried people live with their parents and family members from the father's side, including aunts, uncles, cousins, nieces, nephews and grandparents.

Men and Women

Bangladeshi men are in charge of most parts of society. Bangladeshi women are expected to obey their fathers or husbands. Women have few rights and usually do not have money or own any property. Women have few chances to go to school or to have jobs. In cities, however, some women now have jobs.

Many people follow the Islamic rules of *purdah* (PAWR-dah), which say that after **puberty**, women and men must be separated in social settings. Women and men do not even shake hands in public.

Left: In Bangladesh, some regions follow the rules of purdah more strictly than others do. In some settings, such as at universities, women and men are usually allowed to gather at social events.

Left: Because of the country's traditional values and because of Islamic values, most boys and girls in Bangladesh are not treated equally. Boys have more freedoms in society than girls do.

Children

Almost all Bangladeshi families prefer to have boys. The birth of any child is a happy occasion, though. To keep the baby safe from evil spirits, a good luck charm may be placed around his or her waist. Soot or black makeup is used to make marks on the baby's feet and forehead and around his or her eyes. Most Muslim families **sacrifice** a goat or sheep when the baby is named. The women of the family are in charge of raising the children.

Education

Bangladeshi children are required to attend primary, or elementary, school for five years. However, only about half of them are able to go to school. Many children must work to help support their families or stay home to care for younger children.

After primary school, children may attend secondary school. The schools cost money, so not many can afford to attend. The programme lasts for seven years and is divided into junior, secondary and higher secondary levels.

Left: Children study at their primary school in the rural town of Sunamganj. In many schools, there are too many students and not enough teachers. The government of Bangladesh is now trying to fix this problem.

Madrashas (MAH-drah-shahs), or Islamic schools, provide free education for poor children. The schools house and feed the children, who are taught about the Islamic religion. People give money to help support the schools.

Bangladesh has several universities and many colleges. Some colleges offer courses in subjects such as law, the arts, farming and engineering. Well-known universities include Rajshahi University and Chittagong University. Most people who attend universities are wealthy.

Religion

Hinduism used to be the main religion of Bangladesh. After the late 1800s, Islam became the main religion. In 1988, Islam was declared the country's official religion. Today, most people in Bangladesh are Muslims. Some people are Hindus. A few Bangladeshis are Christians or Buddhists or belong to **animistic** religions. Most often, people from the different religions get along.

Below:
Worshippers crowd the Baitul Mukarram Mosque in Dhaka during a major Muslim festival. A mosque is a Muslim house of worship.

Left: A man stands guard at a Hindu festival. Because some Muslims and Hindus fight, it is often necessary for security forces to protect people at large Hindu events.

Islam and Hinduism

Muslims are divided into two branches of Islam, the Sunnis and the Shi'ites. In Bangladesh, most Muslims are Sunnis. Most Muslims do not eat pork or drink alcohol. They try to pray five times a day. During each day of Ramadan, the Islamic holy month, Muslims do not eat until after sunset. Most villages have a mosque and a Muslim religious leader.

Below: Buddhist monks lead a special prayer session in Dhaka. There are temples and monasteries, which are homes for monks, in Chittagong and Cox's Bazar. Few Bangladeshis are Buddhist, however.

Hindus believe people die and are reborn. They also worship many gods and goddesses. To Hindus, cows are holy, so most Hindus do not eat beef.

Language

The official language of Bangladesh is Bangla, which is also called Bengali. It is spoken by almost all Bangladeshis. Some words from Portuguese, English, Arabic, Hindi and Farsi are included in Bangla. Many Bangladeshis speak a little English, but well-educated people are usually the only ones who speak it well. Nearly 40 other languages are spoken in the country, including Garo, Arakanese, Chittagonian, Sadri, Santali, Chakma, Sylhetti and Tippera.

Left: News-stands in Bangladesh sell daily newspapers in both English and Bangla. Several English magazines are also sold.

Literature

Storytelling is an important part of the culture of Bangladesh. As far back as 2 BCE, artists painted pictures of stories on cloth. The storyteller hung the story picture nearby and often performed the tale by singing, dancing or miming it. Many of the stories were about princes, princesses or fairies. Poet Rabindranath Tagore (1861–1941) is a very famous Bengali author. He won the Nobel Prize for Literature in 1913. Another famous author in Bangladesh is Kazi Nazrul Islam. He is known as the "**rebel** poet".

Arts

Traditional Music

Traditional Bangladeshi music includes classical and folk music. In Bangladesh, classical music is based on the Indian system of tones. It sounds different from Western classical music. Folk music is played on instruments such as the *dotara* (DOH-tah-rah), a four-stringed instrument and the *mandara* (MAHN-dah-rah), which are small cymbals.

Left: The tabla (TAH-blah), which is a pair of drums, is an important musical instrument in Indian classical music.

Dance and Drama

Classical Bangladeshi dance has been influenced by Indian styles of dance and by folk and **tribal** dances from Bangladesh itself. *Dhali* (DHAH-lee) and *manipuri* (MOH-nee-poo-ree) are two famous folk dances in Bangladesh.

Theatre is a popular art form in the country. *Jatra* (JAH-trah) is a type of folk drama that is performed mainly in villages, often during fairs or harvest festivals. Traditional folklore or **myths** are often acted out. Music and dance are usually performed with jatra.

Above: These men and women are performing a dance about catching fish. The women are wearing traditional saris, which are pieces of cloth that are wrapped around the body to form a skirt and a covering for the shoulder or head.

Architecture

Bangladesh's architecture is a mix of styles brought to the country, including Buddhist and Hindu temples, Islamic mosques and European-style churches. In the 1900s, Western-style buildings became popular. Since then, in Dhaka, many apartment buildings have been built to house the growing population. Many poor people in Bangladesh live in homes made of dried mud, brick or bamboo.

Below: These village homes were built in the countryside. Many homes have roofs made from natural materials, such as leaves or straw, or from sheets of metal. Because flooding is very common, many homes are built on stilts or wooden platforms.

Left: Finely embroidered quilts are a traditional form of needlework in Bangladesh. This style of embroidery dates back hundreds of years and began when women recycled their old saris by making them into quilts.

Museums

Bangladesh has many museums. The National Museum was opened in 1913. The museum includes displays of local history, natural history and the history of people around the world. It also has displays of art, including classical art, folk art, decorative art and modern art. **Archaeological** museums are located in Mainamati, Lalbagh Fort, Paharpur, and Mahasthangarh. In Rangamati, displays of costumes and other items made by Bangladeshi groups can be seen at the Tribal Cultural Museum.

Leisure

Bangladeshis enjoy spending leisure time with family, friends and visitors. Most Bangladeshis are very polite to guests and almost always offer them a drink, even if it is just cold water. In Bangladesh, it is improper for a guest to sit on the floor. A common greeting in the country is "*Salaam aleykum*" (sah-LAAM ah-LIE-koom), which means "Peace be unto you".

Below: Bangladeshi children in a rural region skip rope. Many rural children still play traditional games, including skipping rope. In cities, however, such traditional games are no longer popular.

Left: Men relax and enjoy hot tea at a tea stall in Dhaka. Most tea stalls sell hot, sweet, milky tea and biscuits. Many men go to tea stalls during their breaks from work to meet up with friends.

Most of Bangladesh's cities are very crowded, so some Bangladeshis visit the country's many small parks to relax. They often buy food from stalls outside the parks and listen to musicians play. Many women enjoy walking. Younger people play football or traditional games, such as spinning tops or flying kites.

In recent years, several theme parks have been built in Bangladesh, but only middle-class and wealthy people can afford to visit them. Bangladeshis also enjoy watching films, television and plays and going to music concerts.

Left: A Bangladeshi cricket player, Alok Kopali *(left)*, swings his bat. Sri Lanka's players, Prasanna Jayawardena *(centre)* and Hashan Thilakaratne *(right)* look on. The two teams were playing their second Test match in Colombo, India, in July 2003.

Sport

Many Bangladeshis enjoy sport. The country's government supports many sports, especially team sports, such as football and field hockey. Badminton is one of the only sports that Bangladeshi women play. The sport of wrestling is enjoyed mostly by young men.

Many Bangladeshis enjoy watching or playing **cricket**. The team played its first Test match in 2000. Test matches are the world's most respected form of cricket competition. In 2005, the team defeated Zimbabwe in its first ever Test match victory.

Kabaddi

Kabaddi (KAH-bah-dih), the national sport of Bangladesh, is played with two teams of seven players. In the first part, each player tries to touch as many of the other team's players as possible. Players who have been touched are out of that part of the game. In the second part, one player from the winning team runs into the other team's side of the court saying "kabaddi". He must touch as many of the other team's players as he can and run back, all in one breath.

Left: A kabaddi player tags out a player from the other team. Many games of kabaddi include several first and second parts. Players tagged out during the second part cannot play in later rounds. The game is over when one whole team is tagged out.

Religious Festivals

The main festivals in Bangladesh are religious. *Eid-ul-Fitr* (EED-uhl-FIT-er) is the most celebrated Muslim festival. Muslims receive gifts, visit family and wear new clothes. *Eid-ul-Azha* (EED-uhl-AZ-hah) is a Muslim festival held during the time of *hajj* (HAW), which is a **pilgrimage** Muslims try to make to Mecca, in Saudi Arabia, at least once. Hindus celebrate *Durga Puja* (DUR-gah POO-jah) by praying to the goddess Durga. Buddhists celebrate the festival of Buddha Purnima. It honours the birth, **enlightenment** and death of Buddha.

Left: A Bangladeshi girl looks out over a crowd of Muslims praying during Eid-ul-Fitr. The festival takes place at the end of Ramadan.

National Holidays

Bangladeshis celebrate several national holidays, such as International Mother Language Day on 21 February. The day honours the East Pakistanis' fight to keep Bangla as their language. On 26 March, Independence Day is celebrated. Guns are shot off in the morning. Wreaths are left at the National **Martyrs** Monument in Savar. At night, many buildings are lit up. In mid-April, many Bangladeshis celebrate the Bengali New Year.

Above: Every year on 16 December, many Bangladeshis celebrate Victory Day. It marks the day in 1971 when the Liberation War against West Pakistan ended.

Food

Bangladeshi food is full of flavour. It usually includes many spices, such as cloves, coriander and cinnamon. For breakfast, many people eat *ruti* (ROO-tee), which is a round flatbread. The largest meal of the day is lunch, which almost always includes rice and one or more **curry** dishes. The curry often has vegetables and meats such as chicken, fish or beef in it. Like many Muslims, Bangladeshis pick up and eat food with their right hands without using utensils.

Left: A man cooks parata (POH-rah-tah), which is a kind of flatbread, at a food stall. Flatbreads such as parata, ruti, and naan (NAHN) are often eaten at meals instead of rice.

Korma (KOR-mah) is a mildly spicy curry that is popular in Bangladesh. It is made with meat, such as chicken or lamb. The sauce is made of yogurt and ghee, a kind of butter. *Daal* (DAHL) is a thick soup made of lentils, onions, and tomatoes. It is spiced with garlic, turmeric, cinnamon and cilantro.

Many Bangladeshi desserts are made with rice, including *sandesh* (SHOHN-desh), which is made from rice, milk, sugar, nuts and cardamom, a spice.

Cha (CHAH), or tea, is Bangladesh's national drink. It is usually served hot with sugar and milk. *Lassi* (LAHS-sih) is a favourite drink made from yogurt.

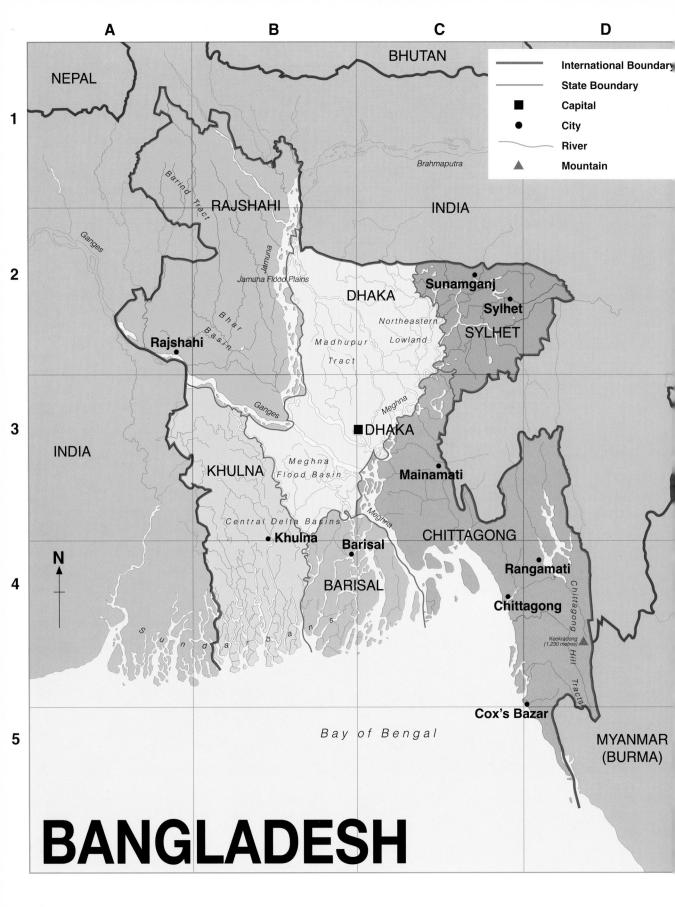

Above: Drivers park rickshaws, or carts pulled by people, outside a busy market area.

Barind Tract A1–B2

Barisal (region)
    B3–C4

Bay of Bengal
    B5–D5

Bhar Basin B2

Bhutan B1–D1

Brahmaputra (river)
    B2–D1

Central Delta
    Basins B3

Chittagong (city) C4

Chittagong Hill
    Tracts D4–D5

Chittagong (region)
    C2–D5

Cox's Bazar D4

Dhaka (city) B3–C3

Dhaka (region)
    B2–C3

Ganges (river)
    A1–B3

India A1–D4

Jamuna Flood
    Plains B2

Keokradong D4

Khulna (city) B3

Khulna (region)
    A3–B4

Madhupur Tract
    B2–C2

Mainamati C3

Meghna Flood
    Basin B3

Meghna (river)
    C2–C4

Myanmar D3–D5

Nepal A1

Northeastern
    Lowland C2

Padma B3–C3

Rajshahi (region)
    A1–B3

Rangamati D4

Sunamganj C2

Sundarbans A4–B4

Sylhet (city) C2

Sylhet Hills C2–D2

Sylhet (region) C2–D2

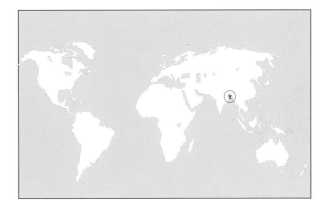

Quick Facts

Official Name People's Republic of Bangladesh

Capital Dhaka

Official Language Bangla (Bengali)

Population 147,365,352 (2006 estimate)

Land Area 144,000 square kilometres

Regions Barisal, Chittagong, Dhaka, Khulna, Rajshahi, Sylhet

Highest Point Keokradong (1,230 metres)

Coastline 580 kilometres

Major Cities Chittagong, Khulna, Cox's Bazar, Sylhet, Dhaka

Major Rivers Brahmaputra, Ganges, Meghna

Main Religion Islam

Religious Festivals *Eid-ul-Fitr, Eid-ul-Azha, Durga Puja, Buddha Purnima*

National Holidays International Mother Language Day (21 February), Independence Day (26 March), Victory Day (16 December)

Currency Taka (86.55 Taka = 1 Euro in May 2006)

Opposite: Many fruits and vegetables grown in Bangladesh are sold at this market.

Glossary

animistic: related to a belief that all things in nature have spirits.

appellate: related to a court in which cases are heard and tried over again.

archaeological: related to studying old items left by people from long ago.

basin: land that is drained by a river and a system of connected streams.

caste: social classes Hindus have been traditionally divided into.

cricket: a game somewhat like baseball.

curry: a food, dish, or sauce made with curry powder or other strong spices.

deltas: flat plains of sand and mud left by rivers when they empty into a sea.

dynasty: a series of rulers who rule over a long time and are from one family.

empire: a very large collection of lands or regions ruled by one group.

enlightenment: related to understanding or having deep knowledge of an idea.

ethnic: related to a race or culture that has similar customs and languages.

export (v): to sell and ship products to other countries.

legislative: related to making laws.

liberation: the act of setting free.

martyrs: people who die or suffer rather than give up their religion or beliefs.

monsoon: a strong, seasonal wind that sometimes brings heavy rains.

mutiny: a fight against those in control.

myths: stories explaining natural events or a group's beliefs.

pilgrimage: a journey made to a holy place as an act of religious devotion.

puberty: the stage at which boys and girls first start to develop sexually.

rebel: a person who fights against a ruler or government.

rural: related to the countryside.

sacrifice (v): to offer a valuable thing, often an animal or person, to a god.

subtropical: related to areas bordering tropical regions but that are not quite as hot or as damp.

traditional: regarding customs or styles passed down through the generations.

tribal: related to groups of people from the same family, nation or race.

tropical: related to very warm and wet regions where plants grow all year.

More Books to Read

Bengal Tiger. Animals Under Threat series. Louise A. Spilsbury, Richard Spilsbury (Heinemann Library)

The Ganges. A River Journey series. Rob Bowden (Hodder Wayland)

Islam. World Beliefs and Cultures series. Sue Penney (Heinemann Library)

Bangladesh: Living in series. Ruth Thomson (Franklin Watts)

Bangladesh. Country Files series. Ian Graham (Franklin Watts)

Bangladesh. Letters From Around the World series. David Cumming (Cherrytree Books)

Websites

www.oxfam.org.uk/coolplanet/kidsweb/world/bangladesh/index.htm

www.panoramaproductions.net/tours/bangladesh/tour.html

Due to the dynamic nature of the Internet, some websites stay current longer than others. To find additional websites, use a reliable search engine with one or more of the following keywords to help you locate information about Bangladesh. Keywords: *Bengal, Chittagong, Cox's Bazar, Dhaka, Ganges, Sundarbans*.

Note to parents and teachers

Every effort has been made by the Publishers to ensure that these websites are suitable for children, that they are of the highest educational value, and that they contain no inappropriate or offensive material. However, because of the nature of the Internet, it is impossible to guarantee that the contents of these sites will not be altered. We strongly advise that Internet access is supervised by a responsible adult.

Index